Hipster
Haiku

Also by Siobhan Adcock

30 Things Everyone Should Know How to Do Before Turning 30

Hipster
Haiku

SIOBHAN ADCOCK

BROADWAY BOOKS
New York

BROADWAY

PUBLISHED BY BROADWAY BOOKS

Published in the United States by Broadway Books, an imprint of
The Doubleday Broadway Publishing Group, a division of
Random House, Inc., New York.
www.broadwaybooks.com

BROADWAY BOOKS and its logo, a letter B bisected on the diagonal,
are trademarks of Random House, Inc.

Book design by Michael Collica
Illustration by Jane Archer

Library of Congress Cataloging-in-Publication Data
Adcock, Siobhan.
Hipster haiku / Siobhan Adcock.— 1st ed.
p. cm.
1. Haiku, American. I. Title.

PS3619.I58H57 2006
811'.6—dc22
2006042517

ISBN-13: 978-0-7679-2373-6
ISBN-10: 0-7679-2373-1

PRINTED IN THE UNITED STATES OF AMERICA

1 3 5 7 9 10 8 6 4 2

[FIRST EDITION]

Introduction

I started writing these haiku, mostly in this tattered spiral-bound journal I've had for years, in between pouring drinks at the bar where I work (I'm not going to name it here because, hello, the place would be instantly swamped) and at the coffeehouse where I hang out every afternoon.* I don't know exactly why I started . . . Mostly

---

*None of this is true. I am not a bartender. I am actually a giant robot made of lions.

because I felt like I had some important issues to explore that I couldn't talk about in my blog. But over time, as the syllables collected, I found myself writing with a real sense of urgency. Who if not me would write about all the yuppies moving into my neighborhood and totally ruining it? Who if not me would write about the things that mattered—the artistic moment our generation is creating right now, under the radar of the mainstream? Who if not me would write poems for people who hate posers and care about art and community and drugs and know Chloë Sevigny isn't that cool? People who are unpretentious but interested in good design, and hungry for authentic, nonmainstream experiences?

So, like I said, I started writing these haiku in my journal, because haiku are kind of terse and old-school and no-bullshit, like the old Polish guys who used to drink at my bar but for some reason left right around when I started working there. I figured eventually I'd bring the haiku out of the journal and take them to the community— stencil haiku on walls and public spaces around town, or leave cryptic haiku notes for people to find on train seats, or make haiku beer cozies or T-shirts—some kind of grassroots art project. In the end, it was easier to make a Web site. (I also tried writing some other kinds of poetry, but you'll have to check out the Web site for that: HipsterHaiku.com)

Before long, though, other people caught on to the haiku project, and some of the best stuff that was sent to the Web site is collected here, in the last pages of the book. It helped me feel less like I'm completely alone in a world I didn't make. There are other people out there who understand me, and like the CD cover says, I will know them by the trail of dead. And/or their clothing.

I really think we're on to something. I think there might be more of us out there. I hope this book finds them and makes them feel the way I did: Finally, I have a home in the world, and everybody who lives there has a white leather belt and a good haircut. Just like me.

Hipster
Haiku

Pop will eat itself:

Hence, T-shirts with wry slogans

About wry T-shirts

Slow morning at work
I search Insound hopefully
For a new import

Your "neighborhoodie"
Sends a very clear message
Which is: "I'm new here"

I only kissed you
Because I saw the playlists
On your damn iPod

She: rides vintage Schwinn
He: skinny, contrarian
I envy their bond

My sardonic wit

Doesn't translate in e-mail

That's why I'm alone

Hand-rolled cigarettes

You call everything "po-mo"

I think I love you

I can't bear to post.

But I can't bear not to post.

Love hurts, message board.

I've just decided
Freelance videography
A bad career choice

I contribute to
literary magazines.
Via internships.

Aspiring DJ
Spins at Mervyn's on Sundays
Mondays at Payless

Sanitation guys
Don't understand fierce street art:
Picked up on trash night

After my fifth year,
"Philosophy Ph.D."
Didn't sound punk rock

Wicker Park Sunday
If you're not at brunch someplace
You're probably dead

Vans and black dress socks
Worst Frisbee player ever
Did not catch one throw

Extra-small sweater
Reveals a complete lack of
Muscle tone, or fat

"Edgy" neighborhood
A cunning broker preaches
Gentrification

We can only date
If you meet me in Brooklyn
I'm strictly borough

Crafty on the BART
En route to 24th Street
Knitting legwarmers

Coolest subway line?
Below-ground battle royale
L train versus G

Silver Lake, L.A.
Proud nation of renters with
Steep car insurance

What's so bad about
A 347 number?
Why didn't he call?

Online personal:
Seventeen bands I like and
Where I went to school

Ex-boyfriend's worst dig:
"You've never heard of that band?"
Indier-than-thou

We're not together
He was a bike messenger
Wore his chain to bed

Vegetarians

Hard to date on a budget

But really great skin

Sunburn and remorse

Coachella Festival

I did not get laid

While he sleeps, I spy
Ann Coulter on his bookshelf
Slip out quietly

I don't blog daily
Such foolish consistency
Says "I have no life"

Saw Famke Janssen
Post it to Gawker Stalker?
I have a girl crush

Yes, you've heard of me

I had a piece on Salon

My blog's in Feedster

When I said I've "shown"

At that gallery, I meant

"Shown up for work there"

I have a trust fund.
So what? Tons of artists do—
There's no shame in it.

"Latte with soy milk,
But make sure it tastes creamy."
Lady, it's *soy milk*.

"Are you Paul or John?"
Used to be the test. Now it's
"Are you Jack or Meg?"

Urban Outfitters
Like the Minotaur it lurks
In darkness to kill

I read *McSweeney's*
But I think it jumped the shark
With the third issue

That's her—the woman
Who threw a dinner party
With Republicans

The best bands break up

Where have you gone, Jeff Mangum?

We hate Elf Power

Only three labels,

Merge, Sub Pop, and Matador,

Deserve your money

Thanks, Aunt Polly. But
Chili's gift certificates
Are no good to me

Fuck your SUV

My Vespa gets good mileage

You're a dinosaur!

Writ on my tombstone:
"Never bought a Greatest Hits
compilation disc"

A bar's authentic

Only if it contains some

Old Polish guys, drunk

For the love of God

Please, please, please read the memo:

No more trucker caps

Cabbie hats, cocaine:
Everything eighties is new
Again. And again.

I love retro bags,
But draw a line at Le Sac:
They're too trendy now

McEnroe poser
Your terry-cloth wristbands are
Obviously new

I should have kept it
Big bronze lone-star belt buckle
Dad got on golf trip

The French bulldog test:
Women who own them are mod
Men who own them: gay

A gal needs two bags:
A walk-of-shame messenger,
and a hot-shit clutch

Wouldn't be caught dead

In a J.Crew jean jacket

Or critter flip-flops

Metal detectors
Make me doubt the usefulness
Of my wallet chain

Rock my Adidas

(Wes Anderson edition)

Never rock Fila

Your puffy ski vest
Has lift tickets on it. But
mine's from junior high.

I'm a regular

The bartender knows my name

I'm lonely inside

Why are you dancing?
Just stare gravely at the band
Act appropriate

This bar doesn't suck:
You have to know where it is
There isn't a sign

You wore faux-fur pants
And ski goggles in August
Whither, mad burner?

A fun drinking game
Guess which college she went to:
Brown or Oberlin?

My bike accident
Has helped me meet tons of hot
Critical Mass girls

Apple martini?

Are you fucking kidding me?

What do I look like?

Found a great new bar
With cheap classic arcade games!
I forgot to drink.

My guilty pleasure:
Watching La Lohan fuck up.
I can't get enough.

If I'm alone and
Trying to read at the bar,
Don't ask for digits.

Growing his sideburns:
Hangs old-school *Witness* poster
For inspiration

Hours at the mirror
Hair gel, dryer, ten fingers
Can't get hair mussed right

I am the wrong size
Too short for skinny tall jeans
Too ripped for band shirt

Jew-fro to fauxhawk
Yes, it seems impossible
But it can be done

I heart vintage clothes
But yes, I can admit it:
I smell like moth funk

Yes, my hair is streaked.

Yes, it sure is "different."

Yes, yes, Uncle Mike.

Chan Marshall, you fox
Where do you get your lip gloss?
You're always glinty

Found a cool day care
Yo La Tengo at nap time
Baby Miles loves it

Will I look old if
I keep my Friendster page up
and don't use MySpace?

Quest for Jagger Hair,
Circa 1968:
Haven't washed this week.

Jagger Quest Part 2:
Carefully arranged hair on
Pillow every night

Jagger Hair achieved!
Just in time for the Spoon show.
Please don't let it rain.

Closet as hourglass:

The sands shift from studded belts

To collared dress shirts

I love to listen
To pre-dot-com oldster tales:
Art majors with jobs!

Got an eyebrow stud
And traded in my tongue ring
When I turned thirty

Gone, gone are the days
When we spoke derisively
Of nine-to-five jobs.

At CMJ Fest

"If it's too loud, you're too old"

Now I know it's true

He is midtown, but
Loves to call stuff "sick" and "tight."
Bless his little heart.

Twelve-year-old nerdboys
Can have their damn Aqua Teens—
I'm a Strong Bad man.

O, Conor Oberst:
Sexy, impossibly fey
My eyes are bright too

The Suicide Girls:
Undeniably hot, but
Insanely scary

E! alterna-girls:
Sienna, Scarlett, Chloë
You bore me to death

Some pilgrims travel
to the holy land. Some go
to the Pirate Store.

Proudly we unveil

A cocktail whose time has come:

Schlitz and Prosecco

To save your barstool,
Top your beer with a coaster:
Secret Smokers' Code.

Rooftop party rules:

Use a "fire escape spotter"

If you get too drunk

My fantasy bar:
The jukebox is all B-sides
All emo, all night

TrashTalk and PrinkLass
Met IRL. Now the thread's
Fully unsexy.

"Guitarist wanted:

Must love post-Pavement Malkmus

And own your own van"

MC: "Me: Bored, hot.

You: dragon tat, Vans, high noon,

Valencia Street."

It doesn't matter

If you're Ranting or Raving:

We're all assholes here.

"For sale: king mattress.
Only had sex on it once.
Asking 900."

Slaving on my rant:
To make "best of" craigslist, you
must mention ass, cat

"Anybody know
Where I can get a ride to
Burning Man for free?"

Seeking freelance gigs
To make rent, I scroll, hopeful.
Shit. All internships.

I trolled the MCs
And Casual Encounters
Nobody loves me

Want to see my place?
It's furnished with found artwork
Like this traffic light

Coffee-table stacks:
Wallpaper*, The Believer
and Lynda Barry

Sleepless channel surf
Please let *Egg* be on Thirteen
And I swear I'll pledge

Vinyl collection
Original plastic sleeves
Alphabetical

Calvin and Hobbes tat
Phish T-shirt, stink of incense:
Can't rent with this guy

Someone stole my bike
Right in front of my building
But left the basket

Check out my bedroom:
Retro tiki-hut theme with
Nonflammable sheets

Like the vintage lamp?
No, it's not from IKEA.
Drop that catalog.

I had two roommates
Then I quit my job to paint
Now I live with four

You know who should date
In, like, ten years? Frances Bean
And Maddox Jolie!

If there's a bald man
In a Lower East Side bar,
It is David Cross

Moby loves mock-rock:
Every Unicorns show,
I saw that fucker

Spike Jonze, heartbreaker:
Miss Coppola, Karen O . . .
Who's next, scruffy beast?

The best thing about
American Apparel:
Ads like web-cam porn

No one believes me,
But I was in *Dirty Found*
And damn, I looked good

My fancy gay friend
Is secretly intrigued by
my Stitch n Bitch night

At South by Southwest

"It's all about the music."

I'm here for the drugs.

"Now Playing" Duel:
He flashes his—Mitchell Froom.
I lose—The Killers.

Last show or comeback?
With Bob "Drink Up, Kids!" Pollard,
You never can tell

Vice used to be fun
But now it just seems played out
Must be all the smack.

When I go to bars
I use a cool pseudonym:
"I'm Luna Danger!"

Thank you, *ReadyMade*:
Now I have something to do
Sundays, besides nap.

Are you on the list?
I know someone in the band
I can get you in

I know, that's life, but
It sucks to hear songs you love
Selling minivans

It would be cool if
Haruki Murakami
Really talked to cats

Typical weekend:
poker, knitting, catch a show,
watch some old Borat

Late at night, at home
I practice my Bjorn Turoque
With Coheed on 'phones

I know I used to
Buy T-shirts before Threadless,
I just don't know why.

Wait, it's four a.m.
Is that too late for me to
Get into your pants?

If there's one thing that
Makes me want to read the news,
It's *Get Your War On*

You know you've arrived
When you are mentioned in the
Wikipedia

Know what's really fun?
Adopt a Cockney accent
And say "Paul Weller"

Skateboarding couple
Wearing matching Sauconys
Crash! It must be love

Ironic mustache

Does require careful tending

Here's a mini-comb

See that guy right there?
Made a fortune overnight
Pabst Blue Ribbon stock

Sometimes I worry
I'll be the only grandma
With no bicep tat

Above 14th Street

For the first time in two years

Where the fuck am I?

Thick black eyeglass frames
Help me, Elvis Costello
You're my only hope

A pilly hoodie

A fresh pack of Parliaments

And we ride tonight

The Hipster Haiku Contest

With the help of our good friends at the Gotham Writers' Workshop, we came up with a way to invite cool kids from Bushwick to Echo Park to lift their voices and rise up and sing as one, to the extent that ever happens outside of an Arcade Fire show. The contest guidelines can be viewed online at HipsterHaiku.com, and they include obscure directives about punctuation, grandmothers, and Dr. Scholl's exercise sandals.

Hundreds of smartypantses with an affinity for retro-modern poetic forms rose to the challenge and sent in their haiku, and we're proud as all get-out to present herewith the cream of the bunch, our winner and finalists.

THE WINNER

I took the records
Your nest of vinyl imports
Try to replace us

Patricia Bailey (Klamath Falls, OR)

THE FINALISTS

He wears the tight jeans
My new crush, the Scrabble champ—
Painfully awkward

Lia Davis (Austin, TX)

It's Tuesday; Tar Beach
Coppertone and Maybelline
I'll risk getting burned

Beth Lowell (Morristown, NJ)

You sound really cute.
I will be able to tell
Once my bangs are cut.

Ashley Macknica (New York, NY)

It was the winter
Of my discontent that I
Grew that Fu Manchu

Frank Merlino (Plano, TX)

I got a tattoo.
I got another tattoo.
I am so tattooed.

Peggy Nelson (Garfield, TX)

Now that we've gone live
With our clever little blog
Fame and fortune wait

B Newman (San Francisco, CA)

My roommate's band is
Experimental in taste;
Seasoned in failure

Audrey Southgate (New York, NY)

On the loft terrace
Anime T-shirts flutter:
The laundry was closed.

Tracy Taylor (Mission Viejo, CA)

Barista T-shirt
In a Laundromat washer
Whips up chai Tide foam

Heather Van Doren (Toledo, OH)

Acknowledgments

Thank you to the following people: Becky Cole, mayor of Hiptown; Brianne Ramagosa, the sheriff; Andrew Roth, hipness deputy (thus, hiputy); Connie and Gillian Adcock, my esteemed homies; and, in no particular order except alphabetical, Karen Anderson, Janelle Asplund, Ann Buechner, Jenn Chen, Andrew Corbin, John Frost, Jerry Gabriel, Sarah Gerkensmeyer, Theo Hummer, Jecca Hutcheson, Jacob Kalish, Melanie Lefkowitz, Sarah Lefton, Anne Leonard, Megan Mortensen, Patrick Mortensen, Patrick Somerville,

Alex Steele, and Jessica Troy. Thank you all for letting me exploit your superior coolness. And your ideas.

Grateful acknowledgment is made to the following accomplished haiku-ists who sent in contest entries that were so good, we had to call them runners-up. Thanks and a tip of the tam-o'-shanter to all of you.

Ruth Adams (Towson, MD)

Mary Alberque (Portland, OR)

HD Alcaro (Roseland, NJ)

Adhab Al-Farhan

Alexandra Alger

Andrew Allan

Andrew Allen (Kansas City, MO)

Donna Anderson

Emily Anderson (Lakewood, OH)

Julie Ansell (San Francisco, CA)

Jennifer Anthony (San Bruno, CA)

Laurie Apple (Astoria, NY)

Kari Apted (Covington, GA)

Analisa Arnold (Brush Prairie, WA)

Aaron Azlant (San Francisco, CA)

Bruce Ballard (New York, NY)

Todd Barwick (Neenah, WI)

Mae Bates (San Francisco, CA)

Richard Becker (Pasadena, CA)

Liz Berntson (Brooklyn, NY)

Pat Bingham (Pocatello, ID)

Laura Birek (Los Angeles, CA)

Liz Black (Brooklyn, NY)

Gina Blasko

Amy Bleu

Rich Bolton (Knightdale, NC)

Lisa Bottone (Warren, NJ)

Gary Bowers (Phoenix, AZ)

Erin Boyd (Bastrop, TX)

Laurie Brassard (South Portland, ME)

Andre Brown (Westerville, OH)

Marian Brown (Brooklyn, NY)

Elena Brunn (New York, NY)

Jade Budden (Brush Prairie, WA)

Derek Burritt (Hoboken, NJ)

Angela Campigotto (Brooklyn, NY)

Louis Capadona (Belleville, NJ)

Gwynn Carver (Riverside, CA)

Angela Cash (Temecula, CA)

Pamela Cash (Temecula, CA)

Maria Christofferson (Brisbane, Australia)

Iris Chung (Astoria, NY)

Rose Cirillo (New Hartford, NY)

Paul Clemas (Jersey City, NJ)

Meredith Cole (Brooklyn, NY)

Aneesa Davenport (Oakland, CA)

Tony Davino (Seattle, WA)

Rebecca DeRosa (Brooklyn, NY)

Lawren Desai (Winston-Salem, NC)

Troy DeVolld (Studio City, CA)

Peter Dudley (Walnut Creek, CA)

Miles Durrance (Berkeley, CA)

Julie Edmonds (New York, NY)

Cyndi Elliott (Chicago, IL)

Eric Enright (New York, NY)

Hope Estes (Vancouver, WA)

Lynnea Farrey (Brush Prairie, WA)

Mike Fiorito (Brooklyn, NY)

Brook Fischer (Brooklyn, NY)

Barbara Frank (Prairie Village, KS)

Tiffany Funk (Chicago, IL)

Indra Gandy (Staten Island, NY)

Nina Gantcheva (New York, NY)

Delores Garcia (Elmhurst, NY)

Margaret Garcia-Couoh (Crescent Mills, CA)

Rich Gasparre (New York, NY)

Jasper Gauthier (Portland, OR)

Stefan Glidden (Sherman Oaks, CA)

Janessa Goldbeck (Astoria, NY)

James Gonzales

Reggie Gonzales (Los Angeles, CA)

Drew Greco (Wantagh, NY)

Eirik Gumeny (Nutley, NJ)

Joy Hae Yung (San Francisco, CA)

Jenn Halley (New York, NY)

Amanda Hamann (Brooklyn, NY)

Philip Harjung (San Francisco, CA)

Colleen Harker

Keri Hellesto (San Diego, CA)

Melinda Hightower (Chattanooga, TN)

Molly Hillstrom (White Salmon, WA)

Fern Hilyard (Pembroke, ME)

Jessica Holmes (New York, NY)

William Hoppins (Los Angeles, CA)

Michele Host (New York, NY)

Joyce Hunt (Saratoga Springs, NY)

Gena Hymowech (Brooklyn, NY)

Carmen Iglesias (New York, NY)

Larissa Jaye (New York, NY)

Teresa Jenkins (Belleville, NJ)

Kristen Jenson (Chesterfield, MO)

Stace Johnson (Federal Heights, CO)

Samantha Johnston (New York, NY)

Allison Joseph (Carbondale, IL)

Amy Kaufman (Alhambra, CA)

Sara Kellner (New York, NY)

David Khalaf (Santa Ana, CA)

Rebecca Kidder (San Francisco, CA)

Michelle Knoetgen (Brooklyn, NY)

Allison Koehler (Stallings, NC)

Abigail Koenig (Brooklyn, NY)

Angie Konstantino (Munster, IN)

Tracy Koretsky (Berkeley, CA)

Kathryn Kreimer (Portland, OR)

Bryan Kruse (Brooklyn, NY)

Anna Kutulas (Petaluma, CA)

Brian Laesch (West Hollywood, CA)

Matt LeBoeuf

Renee Levene (Atlanta, GA)

Robin Levine (Los Angeles, CA)

Oliver Libaw (Brooklyn, NY)

Virginia Lloyd (New York, NY)

Amani Ellen Loutfy (Seattle, WA)

Carisa Lubeck (Oakland, CA)

Sheridan MacAuley (Arlington, VA)

Shannon Malloy (San Francisco, CA)

Nick Mamatas (Brattleboro, VT)

Dena Martin (Pasadena, CA)

Meghan McFadden (Renton, WA)

NPB McQuown (New York, NY)
Michael McTigue (Philadelphia, PA)
Elizabeth Meggs (Brooklyn, NY)
Dara Miles (New York, NY)
Leanna Miles (The Woodlands, TX)
Melissa Miles (Alameda, CA)
Scott Miles (The Woodlands, TX)
Josh Miller (Bend, OR)
Shari Mislin (Sterling Heights, MI)
Chris Morin (Saskatoon, Canada)
Hollee Morrow (Avondale, AZ)
Carey Myles (Portland, OR)
Laura Nathan (Buffalo, NY)
Adrienne Neff (Marblehead, MA)
Karen Newman (New York, NY)
Missy Nolan
Corrinne Oedekerk (Bend, OR)
Bryan O'Neill (Seattle, WA)
Theresa O'Reilly (New York, NY)
Katy Orr (Belmont, CA)
Roger Ost (Seattle, WA)
Alison Parkhurst (Wichita, KS)
Gordon Petry (Pekin, IL)
Jennifer Prediger (Washington, DC)

Pratiba Premkumar (New York, NY)
Joanna Prisco (Brooklyn, NY)
Aliene Pylant (Flower Mound, TX)
Julianne Quinn (Houston, TX)
Stephanie Rabiner (Culver City, CA)
Helen Rafferty (Mamaroneck, NY)
Amy Raphael (Jersey City, NJ)
Jodie Rodriguez (San Francisco, CA)
Lola Rodriguez (Sunnyside, NY)
Sarah Royal (Lebanon, NJ)
Delores Rubin (New York, NY)
Martin Sacchetti (Albany, NY)
Allison Schultz (New York, NY)
Erika Schwartz (Brooklyn, NY)
Amanda Scott (New York, NY)
Jeremy Sharp (Bodega Bay, CA)
Bonnie Shaw (Melbourne, Australia)
John Sheppard (Charlotte, NC)
Corinna Sherman (Jersey City, NJ)
Lukas Sherman (Portland, OR)
Jonathan Shipley (Vashon, WA)
Laura Silk (Philadelphia, PA)

Mona Singh (Cambridge, MA)

Chris Smiley (Middlesex, England)

Allison Sommers (New York, NY)

A Song (New York, NY)

Michelle Spriegel (Puyallup, WA)

Ken Stec (New York, NY)

Mia Stendahl (Dublin, NH)

Kate Stepanski (San Francisco, CA)

Justin Stewart (Tempe, AZ)

Renee Stock (Chicago, IL)

Rich Stone (New York, NY)

Jeffrey Stout (Eugene, OR)

E Summers (Boynton Beach, FL)

Katie Tandy (Brighton, MA)

Janet Taylor (Colleyville, TX)

Rachael Taylor (Straffordsville, Canada)

Jayni Therkildsen (Santa Fe, NM)

Katoria Tinsley (Gwynn Oak, MD)

Cassandra Tondreau (Seattle, WA)

Ann Tufariello (Chatham, NJ)

Rachel Turner (San Francisco, CA)

Melanie VanLyssel (Albuquerque, NM)

Karen Walcott (New Paltz, NY)

Shari Wald (Brooklyn, NY)

Zachary Waldman (New York, NY)

Alex Wasowicz (Santa Barbara, CA)

Wendy Watkins (Brewer, ME)

Bob Weir (Webster, NY)

Rachel Weshnak (Kew Gardens, NY)

Michael Whalen (Austin, TX)

Helen White (New York, NY)

Stella Whitlock (Fayetteville, NC)

Danielle Widman (Amherst, OH)

Brooke Williams (New Albany, OH)

Hazel Wilcox (Mammoth Spring, AR)

Noelle Wilson (Silver Spring, MD)

Sabrina Wonsowicz (Staten Island, NY)

Kenneth C. Wonsowicz Jr. (Staten Island, NY)

Kelly Wright (Brookfield, CT)

Margery Yaeger (Washington, DC)

Casey Yarboe (Los Angeles, CA)

James Yeh (San Francisco, CA)